DEVON'S WATERWAYS

Acknowledgements

The author and publishers wish to thank the following for permission to use their copyrighted photographs. Mr I.H. Farquarson-Coe, R.L. Knight and the Devon County Council Tourist Department.

© James Pike Ltd

First Edition 1974

ISBN 0 85932 081 2

**Printed by Sawtell & Nielson Ltd
Newton Abbot, Devon.**

DEVON'S WATERWAYS

by A. Farquharson-Coe

VIEWING
DEVON
SERIES

JAMES PIKE LTD

St. Ives, Cornwall, England

Devon

- Lynmouth
- Ilfracombe
- Barnstaple
- Bideford
- South Moulton
- Tiverton
- Holsworthy
- Honiton
- Okehampton
- EXETER
- Exmouth
- Tavistock
- Newton Abbot
- Totnes
- Torquay
- PLYMOUTH
- Dartmouth
- Brixham

Somerset

Cornwall

Devon's Waterways

In common with the Almighty, Devon has "a thousand sparkling rills" - if not more, some navigable rivers and some famous fishing rivers, but, probably because of its extensive sea-board, both north and south, and the navigable rivers we mentioned, only a few canals. There are no natural lakes but several man made reservoirs; in short, whatever the water boards may say, Devon has a considerable amount of water.

All the little streams of Devon, when they run in their natural surroundings, are pleasant to look at, linger by and listen to. There is the little Lumburn river in the south, meandering along and forming the boundary of the Tavistock abbot's corn lands at his ancient manor of Parswell. There is the Welcombe river quietly moving through dim woodlands before splashing over a little waterfall into the wild seas of the rocky North Devon coast. Between these two there are countless little brooks feeding the larger streams or finding their own far from weary way safe to sea.

To learn something of Devon's rivers we could start at the beginning of the county as it were, at the eastern boundary of the south coast of Devon, and at the beginning of the alphabet, with the river Axe and its tributaries, the Yarty and the Coly. The Yarty gets its name from the wagtails which flickered up and down the stream in the days of our Anglo Saxon forefathers in the same delightful way in which they haunt it today. The old name for wagtail was earte. The wagtails' stream is still well worth exploring up to Yarcombe, a very delightful village near the Somerset boundary. Axe of course is not entirely a Devon river as it has

The dam at the Burrator Reservoir

its source in Somerset, but most of it is in Devon. Winding through pleasant pastoral scenery it is joined by the Yarty just below Axminster, and by the Coly not far from Seaton.

Having made a beginning we look farther west and immediately we abandon any alphabetical pretensions for the sake of contiguity and introduce the little river Sid which enters the sea through its shingly bank thrown up by the tide, at the delightful resort of Sidmouth beloved of Queen Victoria's father who lived with his family at a house called "The Glen" on the esplanade, and died there from a chill caught, it was said, by over vigorous exercise. Sidmouth was the most important resort in South Devon in those days before Torquay rose in popularity, but for all their efforts the inhabitants could not build themselves a harbour, or even a pier. The winter waves always defeated them and in the end they gave up. The Sid makes a westward boundary to a triangle which could have the valley of the Axe for its other side and the pleasant coast from Sidmouth to Seaton for its base. For a family holiday, providing pebbled beaches, (and a little sand at Sidmouth) for the children, fishing for father, and pleasant towns, inland as well as coastal for entertainment and holiday shopping for mother, and the most beautiful scenery, particularly inland, for everyone, it would be most difficult to beat this most Devonshire of Devon holiday districts. There is history; a daughter of King Edward the Fourth is buried at Colyton. Ashe House is believed by some to be the birthplace of the famous Duke of Marlborough, and, if we are looking for even more remote history, a British camp existed at Musbury, while midway in the ages comes the claim of Seaton to be a Roman settlement.

The river Otter, with one of Devon's most beautiful inland towns, Ottery St. Mary, on its banks, flows into the sea at Otterton. Exploration of this area can be combined with that in the Exeter - Exmouth district. Its upper waters however, especially near the beautiful village of Upottery can be visited on an excursion to the head waters of the Yarty, the ridge of Stockland Hill dividing the two valleys. Lovers of English poetry may care to combine a visit to the river at Ottery St. Mary with a pilgrimage to St. Mary's Church, where Coleridge's father was vicar, and to the old grammar school where he taught. Thackeray lived here for a time in his youth and Ottery St. Mary is immortalised as

Clavering St. Mary in one of his novels. As a small boy Coleridge spent many hours by the riverside, and a sandy cave in its banks used to be shown as a favourite refuge of his.

Returning to the coast and going westward, Exmouth, with its outlet for the river Exe with its many important tributaries, the Culm, the Kenn, and the Clyst among them, is better taken with Exeter. Topsham, on the estuary of the Exe can boast of the first canal in England. Running from Topsham to Exeter it was the answer of the city of Exeter to feudal oppression, and will be described later in the section dealing with Devon's canals.

After the Exe, the next river of any size is the Teign. Teignmouth, its estuary town, is a bracing resport famous as a holiday town for generations. It has a harbour at the river mouth where coasters ship the ball clay brought from the Newton Abbot and Bovey Tracey districts. A small stream called the Tame separated East and West Teignmouth many years ago but this has long since been filled in and forgotten. Shaldon, the old world village of sailing ship

Huccaby Bridge, Dartmoor.

days is just across the estuary and has an old smugglers' tunnel through the cliffs. The wooded hills rising to the Dartmoor tors make a very pleasant backcloth for this very pleasant family resort. Teignside provides some beautiful river walks. Fingle Bridge, about five miles upstream is a famous beauty spot. Built of Dartmoor granite it is believed to have been built in the first years of the reign of Elizabeth Tudor, and spans the brawling young river in its deep gorge.

The Teign's tributary, the Bovey, rises on Dartmoor, that birthplace of nearly all Devon rivers, and runs in a deep valley to the plain of Bovey Tracey. Two miles level flow brings it to the Teign. Both rivers are narrow because tributary brooks higher up are scanty. Teign therefore remains a fairly modest stream until Newton Abbot is reached but from there to the sea at Teignmouth it broadens to a wide estuary.

Just along the coast from Teignmouth one comes to Torquay, the resort which springs to mind immediately Devon's coast is mentioned. Rising into popularity during the war with France it became a haven for naval officers' families during those troubled times. Torquay has all the emenities of a popular and fashionable resort while retaining the grace of more leisured days. There are many beautiful and pleasing resorts in Devon, and, indeed in Britain, but there is only one Torquay. Torquay is different.

The fleet sometimes lay up in Torbay, preferring it to Plymouth, but a little distance westward again is the famous port at the mouth of the Dart which might have become the naval base and dockyard instead of Plymouth but for the narrowness of its harbour. Formed from two settlements, Hardness in the north and Clifton on the south side of the river, Dartmouth possesses as its only flat land the reclaimed pool called Mill Pool which ran back for some way inland and separated the two hamlets. Shipping was always the way of life at Dartmouth. Chaucer's "schipman" was probably based on a member of a famous Dartmouth family named Hawley, and its first street to be recorded in local history was Smith Street, - the street of the ship repairers - which, owing to reclamation schemes, now has its being farther away from the shore than formerly. The crusaders used this harbour in the twelfth century and the esteem in which it was held by the knights and shipmasters on those

The River Dart at Totnes.

famous voyages led to the town's formation as a borough in the thirteenth century.

Dartmouth Castle stands on one side of the mouth of the Dart and on the other is Kingswear Castle built in the fifteenth century. Once stout chains spanned the harbour mouth between castle and castle to repel raiders but they have long since gone, and in 1855 Kingswear Castle suffered the indignity of being transformed into a house, and a holiday residence at that.

The Dart Valley provides fascinating rambles. Holne Chase, a beautifully wooded horseshoe shaped glen should certainly be visited. If the literary character is still with us he might like to know that Charles Kingsley was born at Holne Vicarage when his father acted as temporary curate there for a few months. Buckland Beacon, a few miles from Ashburton, provides a magnificent view southwards over the beautiful reaches of the Dart. Here the little Webburn, joining its two little branches, goes on to enter the Dart. Higher up one reaches Poundsgate where there is a prominent tor giving yet another delightful view of the Dart Valley, and a mile or so beyond, one reaches the famous Dartmeet. Boats take visitors from Dartmouth up the river so far as Totnes, an ancient town said to be the oldest town in Devon. Situated on a hill rising from the Dart it is well worth a visit. The first bridge there is believed to have been built before the reign of King John and the last in 1828 by a celebrated Devon architect, Charles Fowler. The Dart from Totnes is a smoothly flowing river with wide pleasant reaches. The wooded estates of Sharpham lie along one bank and from the river glimpses can be caught of Stoke Gabriel's church tower. Dittisham, where the Dart widens to a vast expanse is a port of call for the boats and the Dart then narrows to Lower Gittisham where there is a ferry. Greenway, where Sir Walter Raleigh's half brother, Sir Humphrey Gilbert was born, lies on the left bank of the Dart, and is said to have been the first place to grow a potato in England.

From Dartmouth it is but a short distance to little Stoke Fleming with its church brass to the memory of Elias Newcomen, the great grandfather of Thomas Newcomen of Dartmouth, the Devon-born inventor of the steam engine. From there a descent is made to Start Bay and on to Slapton Sands and the famous Lea. This is a beach of more than two miles in length but rising only a few feet above high water mark. On the landward side is a sheet of fresh water, Slapton Lea, extending from a quarter to half a mile in width. Slapton and the country round it was evacuated and used for practice amphibious landings in 1944 and an obelisk was erected in the middle of the long beach to commemorate the occasion. The wide expanse of water is famous as an ornithologists' paradise. Good catches of coarse fish can also be had there.

Our next river is one of the many Avons in England. Rising at Avon Head on Dartmoor it flows through delightful country reaching its estuary just below Aveton Gifford. This little river, one of the smallest but one of the most beautiful of the Avons, is well worth exploring to its source. It has wooded glens, old bridges and a delightful series of little cascades. Kingsbridge, facing the estuary is well worth a visit. It is a small but interesting town having its beginnings well before the thirteenth century. Kingsbridge is famous as the birthplace of the first person to use china clay for making porcelain in Britain, Thomas Cookworthy, but to tipplers its manufacture of the famous ale said by some to have been the original beverage of our Saxon forefathers, and by others to have been the concoction of a German doctor who once resided here and who brewed it specially for patients with stomach ache, is Kingsbridge's only passport to fame.

The rivers Erme and Yealm come next in our westward journey. Both rise on Dartmoor, not very far from each other, the Erme flowing into Bigbury Bay and the Yealm into Wembury Bay. Both are beautiful rivers, the Erme passing through moorland scenery runs through a narrow ravine through Ivybridge and past Ermington with its softly wooded banks at Holbeton, before reaching the sea at Mothecombe. The Yealm stays near the Erme, although the latter is a fair sized stream before Yealm makes its debut near Shell Tor. Passing through a spectacularly beautiful glen known as Awns and Dendles it flows through typical Devon scenery to Yealmpton. From there, it is but a short distance to the lovely villages of Noss Mayo and Newton Ferrers on opposite shores of what must surely be one of the most beautiful estuaries in Britain.

Most rivers, including all these previously mentioned which have their estuaries on the south Devon coast, pour into the sea under the same names they have borne since they were little brooks. Not so in the case of our last river, the very important Plym which gives its name to Plymouth, for the little Plym has been known as the Cad, with at least one bridge of that name, and its estuary waters are known at Plymouth as the Laira or Lairy. Rising on Dartmoor well into the moor near the quaintly named Great Gnats Head, the Plym winds its way tortuously westward, passing under Gadover Bridge before reaching Shaugh Bridge and its confluence with the Meavy at one of the most picturesque spots in the Bickleigh Vale. Continuing through beautifully wooded country the river becomes a wide smooth beautiful estuary at Plympton, its tidal flats the haunt of innumerable water birds, before it comes to Plymouth and the sea.

We now come to a river, a very important river, and a large one, of which Devon can only claim one bank. Tamar is the boundary between Devon and Cornwall. Although the eastern bank is territorially Devon, the Cornish River Authority administers it and the rivers which flow into it from the Devon side. Tamar was, and to some extent still is, a highway for all the little riverside villages and for those inland as well, but the greatest traffic in comparatively recent times was that of ores from the mines in the Tavistock and Dartmoor areas. The port of Morwellham, now a rather self conscious museum exhibit where tea and tourist souvenirs can be had, handles the traffic from one of the largest and richest copper mines in the world barely a century ago. The Devon Great Consols Mine produced between 1844 and 1878 over three million pounds worth of copper, in the days when a million pounds was a great deal of money.

Not far upstream from Saltash Bridge, Tamar receives its most important tributary, the beautiful river Tavy. Close by is the opening to the Tamar of the Tamerton Lake, a two mile long creek. Tavy rises on Dartmoor near Fur Tor in almost impenetrably boggy country and rushes down past two or three lonely farmsteads and the villages of Cudlipp Town, Mary Tavy and Peter Tavy, to the beautiful and famous little town of Tavistock, birthplace of Sir Francis Drake. The Tavy's principal tributary, the Walkham, joins the Tavy below Horrabridge and the merged rivers empty their waters into the Tamar just above the Tamerton Lake, the sentinel Warleigh Tor superintending this west country meeting of the waters. Very pleasant agricultural country forms the Devon bank of the Tamar, with pleasant little streams flowing into it such as the Lew and the Carey, before reaching its source in the high country of the north.

River Tavy at Tavistock.

The Rivers of North Devon

Near the source of the Tamar rises the Torridge, an equally famous river, having its source and estuary in the north of the county. From its source it flows south through quiet remote farmlands before it is joined by the Walson not far from Black Torrington, then, passing through Sheepwash it curves round through Meath and begins its convoluted course northward, making fantastic loops and bends, until it reaches Great Torrington. Here main road and river accompany each other until Bideford is reached and the Torridge flows past Appledore to join the waters of the Taw in Barnstaple - or Bideford - Bay. If you're a Bideford man then it's Bideford Bay, if a native of Barnstaple, naturally you call it Barnstaple Bay. Most maps are tactful enough to show both names.

River Torridge at low tide, Bideford.

Taw, Barnstaple's river, rises on Dartmoor and makes its pleasant way as soon as it can to the main road and the now disused railway, and accompanies both all the way to Barnstaple. Here it widens into a broad estuary having been augmented by the smaller streams of Bray and Mole and the Little Dart in the South Molton country. The Taw estuary became silted up about the seventeenth century and the scouring action of the tides cleaning the course of the Torridge gave Bideford the maritime trade which formerly belonged to Barnstaple. However, Barnstaple still has some coastal and overseas trade and continues to rank as a customs port.

From Barnstaple the coastline goes north with a west-facing aspect from Braunton Burrows to Bull Point, where it is not far to the Exmoor shores of the Bristol Channel and the mouth of the Heddon river. The Heddon runs through magnificent scenery culminating in its superb entry to the sea. Close by are Combe and Woody Bay, and the tiny villages of Trentishoe and Mortinhoe. Making Barnstaple one's centre, a very pleasant holiday could be spent exploring the valley of the Heddon with its delightful villages, and perhaps taking a trip farther east to the famous holiday places of Lynton and Lynmouth where the two Lyns, East and West, meet to empty themselves into the sea. The scenery of this district, moorland, sea and valley, is world famous. The highlights are Lyn Cleave, dividing the valleys of the two rivers, Lee Abbey, which never was an abbey and is now a hotel; Watersmeet, the Foreland, and the well known Valley of the Rocks, for the strong in nerve best visited by moonlight for the eerie shadow effects.

Reservoirs, Ponds and the like

There are no real lakes in Devon; may be a tarn or two, difficult enough to find, on Dartmoor, but there are several reservoirs which resemble lakes. One of the most well known is the Burrator Reservoir upon which opinions differ and rage. To some it is one of the most beautiful stretches of water imaginable. Others, perhaps more discriminating, may grant the attraction but assert that it is out of place on Dartmoor. There are reservoirs near Bovey Tracey, the Kennick and Tottiford Reservoirs, and Fernworthy Reservoir near Chagford extends to seventyfive acres, a fine piece of water. Ponds near Newton Abbot, including the artificial lake at Stover, amount to seven large expanses and are well worth a visit.

Whistland Pound Reservoir, Simonsbath.

In the north of the county we have the Slade Reservoirs near Ilfracombe, and near Blackmoor Gate on the main Barnstaple-Bideford road there is the Westpoundland Reservoir, while there are three reservoirs in the Bideford area, Gamaton, Jennets and Darracotts.

Slapton Ley on the South coast, as previously mentioned is well worth a visit. It is the property of the Herbert Whitley Trust and, with the surrounding country, forms a nature reserve and bird sanctuary. It is governed by strict rules and obviously these must be adhered to. The address of the Field Warden is Field Centre, Slapton, Kingsbridge.

The Canals in Devon

Exeter Canal

Finally we come to waterways proper, the canals which were constructed in Devon in the eighteenth century during the canal boom, that is, all except the famous one, the sixteenth century canal at Topsham near Exeter. If Roman work is disregarded this Exeter canal is the oldest waterway in Britain, and we can make a start with its history, or so much as we know, for despite many stories, the exact truth of the blocking of the river Exe which necessitated the building of the canal, is not known. The most likely story is that the Countess of Devon, a lady by the name of Isabella de Fortibus, quarrelled with the burgesses of Exeter and built a weir across the Exe, still called Countess Wear, which put an effective stop to boats getting to Exeter. Those may have been feudal days but the Exeter inhabitants weren't putting up with this highhanded action. They went to law and after much litigation a thirty foot gap was made to enable vessels to pass. This rankled in high places until the early years of the fourteenth century when High Courtenay, the then Earl of Devon, not only blocked up the gap in the Countess's weir but added a few more bits of impedimenta of his own including a quay which he built at Topsham where boats were compelled to unload, thereby earning toll charges for the earl. So the Exeter worthies went to law again, but gained nothing but an empty verdict for although they won their case in court, in Exeter they got no farther forward for the earl calmly ignored the court's decision and went on collecting his tolls.

A hundred years later however Hugh Courtenay came to political grief and the Corporation of Exeter seized this opportunity to obtain an Act of Parliament enabling them to remove the obstructions. But with all their efforts they could not make a navigable job of the Exe until the middle of the eighteenth century when they engaged a Welsh engineer to plan a canal for them. He was to have a fairly substantial fee and a percentage of the revenue. Every church in the city, and there were a great many, is said to have contributed a piece of its plate towards the cost of building the new waterway to the sea.

From the Exe, a few hundred yards from the city walls where a quay was built, the canal was planned to run to Matford Brook, avoiding the weirs, a length of little over three hundred yards. From here the river was improved as far as Topsham. The work began in 1564 and was finished in 1566 and it cost the town about £5,000 which included the churches subscription of 500 ounces of silver. A pair of gates was erected at the seaward end and three pound locks were built. The canal took craft of up to sixteen tons, cargoes being transhipped in the estuary. All this was of course a great improvement on the previous position but difficulties began to arise. The estuary was awkward and the waterway was only usable at high tide for boats of any size; and in addition the river had a tendency to silt up in its higher reaches. The remains of feudal opposition still controlling Topsham quay insisted on trying to collect tolls on goods entering the canal even though they were not landed at the quay. An arrangement was then entered into whereby the corporation compounded for the dues by an annual payment, and later the quay was leased to the corporation for thirty years but the lease was not renewed and the quay reverted to the previous owners.

The corporation certainly had some difficult people to

deal with over the canal. After the Civil War an attempt was made to improve the waterway which had fallen into a semi derelict state and it was found that a woollen merchant had taken advantage of the hostilities to cut a channel to his mill at Exeter from the river. The corporation soon dealt with him, but the Topsham quay wrangle still continued. In 1676 the canal was properly dredged and extended a further half mile towards Topsham to bypass a bad piece of river. A larger entrance was constructed to take sixty ton vessels and a quay and another weir were built at Exeter. In 1691 the canal had become so profitable that the corporation decided to enlarge it once more. This time they intended it to take seagoing craft but unfortunately their contractor decamped with the money before the work was completed. With praiseworthy energy the men and women of Exeter flocked to the canal to help to finish it. More money was borrowed, and the intrepid Exonians reopened their canal in 1701. Ten feet deep and fifty feet wide it could accommodate craft of up to a hundred and fifty tons.

Double locks were substituted for the old locks and the lower pound became a long lock with a rise of four feet. Further work was necessary to increase the level of the lower pound, and this was undertaken. In 1821 the canal was dredged and straightened after over a hundred years of prosperity. James Green the famous canal engineer undertook this work and in 1824 he recommended an extension of the canal a further two miles down the river. This was done and the banks of the canal raised to increase the depth of water. A proper basin was constructed at Exeter and the whole of the work, including a side lock to placate the opposition at Topsham, was completed by 1832.

The serge trade in Devon was killed by the wars, although it was a fairly long time a-dying but although the carriage of a miscellaneous collection of goods compensated to some degree for this, the balance was not maintained, and when the railway came to Exeter with the opening of the Bristol and Exeter line in 1844 the canal traffic was seriously affected. In an effort to maintain some measure of prosperity the dues were lowered but things became more and more difficult, and although the lessors who had taken over the canal from the corporation, would have accepted the new steam traffic on the canal the corporation forbade the use of the waterway by steam boats under their own power and insisted that they should be towed by horses on account of possible damage to the banks. The new railways, with loading facilities at South Devon ports took most of the trade from Exeter, the canal traffic decreasing proportionately, until the control of the canal reverted to the corporation in 1883.

Exeter Corporation still owns and runs its canal for which it fought so many years ago, although the traffic upon it is now mainly oil and timber.

Lord Rolle's Canal at Torrington

It is today's practice to disparage what are referred to as the bad old days, but there is much to be said for them. In 1823 Lord Rolle and his engineer, James Green, took and started a canal of their own without filling in the tiniest little application form or obtaining permission from the most junior planning officer or his nineteenth century equivalent. They began it with a lock and basin adjoining the Torridge near Weare Giffard just under two miles above Bideford Bridge. Running beside the river for the better part of a mile the canal reached its summit level by a single inclined plane. Powered by a waterwheel it took small tub boats fitted with wheels and reaching Beam it traversed the river by means of an aqueduct. Here Lord Rolle really let himself go. He built a fine classically designed aqueduct with five rounded arches to carry his canal across the Torridge. The canal then followed the river from its other bank to the limekilns at Taddiport and to its terminus at New Manor Mill, a mile beyond Great Torrington, a distance of about six miles.

Coal and limestone from Wales shipped to Bideford or Appledore provided most of the traffic for his lordship's little canal, which was opened in 1827 with the passage of a vessel from Bristol laden with coal which was to be distributed among the poor of Torrington as a gift from Lord Rolle to commemorate the occasion. From the entrance lock her cargo was to be transferred to smaller boats which were to "proceed to the town of Torrington" via the inclined plane and the "beautiful and substantial stone aqueduct".. Already a shipbuilding yard had been established at the beginning of the canal and the company built its own vessels there. A schooner of ninetyeight tons was the first craft to be built and was duly named "The Lord Rolle" Threemasters of up to two hundred tons burthen were built at the little yard but with the increasing use of steam and the economic conditions of the times, the shipbuilding gradually decreased and the yard eventually closed in 1870. Approximately in 1871 the little canal followed suit, although the exact date of its closure is not known. Lord Rolle's beloved stone aqueduct became a private drive at Beam, the railway bisected the inclined plane and the rest of the canal was abandoned.

The Stover Canal

James Templer, the respected squire of Stover House. Teigngrace, began life as a joiner's apprentice in the city of Exeter in the eighteenth century, found life boring and ran away to sea. Somehow he found himself in India, still a young man. Here he became what we would now call a public works contractor, and obtained a contract to build the docks at Madras. Returning to England he was awarded further public contracts and enriched both in pocket and reputation he looked around for a country seat in his native county. He found himself a derelict estate about two miles from Teigngrace, with a ruined mansion house. Half a mile from the ruined house he built himself a new mansion, Stover House, and began to build himself a canal.

Originally he intended to take his canal to Bovey Tracey through Jewsbridge and Heathfield, extending a branch to Chudleigh, but having reached Ventiford he built his clay cellars there and went no farther, although he applied to parliament for permission to raise further moneys by mortgage should such a step be needed, having spent his own money until then. To the Templer family, father and son, the Teign valley owed much of its prosperity in those days.

Only small hamlets and villages existed in the area then and the transport needs had to be assessed on an industrial basis from the beginning. The fine ball clay which was being extracted in the area in the 1730's had to be carted from the pits to Newton Abbot along rough trackways, then shipped down the Teign. Excessive handling proved wasteful in time and transport costs. From the clay carts the substance was loaded into barges for its journey down the river; these carried a maximum of thirty tons each, and when Teignmouth was reached the clay had to be loaded into ships for the Mersey ports and the potbanks of the midlands, necessitating yet a third handling before the clay left Devon. All this inefficiency was too much for James Templer. He engaged an engineer, Thomas Gray of Exeter, and got to work. Starting in 1790 he built his canal with a pair of locks near the entrance and three others higher up. Except for the graving dock lock, all of them could take two barges in line, the lowest lock being enlarged eventually to 215 feet by 45 feet. The Teign was joined at Newton Abbot at Jetty Marsh and great was the local rejoicing when the waterway was opened.

Almost at once the canal became busy, much of the traffic being Templer's. The barges were rigged with the last survival in Britain of the ancient Viking seagoing rig and were sailed or bowhauled by tough characters mostly from the Kingsteignton district. The canal remained busy and prosperous and in September 1820 James Templer's son George added further traffic with granite from the Templer quarries at Hey Tor. Awarded a contract to provide granite for public works in London which began with London Bridge and later included the General Post Office, the British Museum and the National Gallery, he constructed a tramway from Hey Tor to Ventiford and afterwards built the New Quay at Teignmouth for greater convenience in loading the clay and granite, which hitherto had been transhipped in midriver. By 1829 however, the Templer sun had began to set and the canal and its railway were eventually sold to the Duke of Somerset.

Further improvement of the harbour facilities at Teignmouth were undertaken in 1836 and work done on the Teign as far as its junction with the canal. The still flourishing trade in ball clay had resulted in the Hackney canal being built by Lord Clifford. This little canal, a hundred or so yards short of threequarters of a mile in length, reached from the Teign to the Newton Abbot-Kingsteignton road, and was opened in March 1843. Both canals benefitted by work done by the river authorities in staking river channels in the Teign. However, railways had entered the transport world and although the clay trade provided 100,000 tons of traffic in 1905 most of which was carried by water, first the railways, then road transport gradually obtruded themselves until the canals of the Teign valley fell into disuse; the Hackney in 1928, and, although several barges still worked the canal in 1931, the Stover followed its little neighbour in 1939.

The Crediton Canal Schemes

There were two of these; the first came to very little, and the second began, and ended, in what is now described as "meaningful dialogue".

The universal canal boom doubtless inspired the group of Exeter businessmen who considered that an extension of the canal system to Crediton would benefit the country, and no doubt themselves, to put forward a proposal for a canal to run from Four Mills at Crediton to the River Exe, joining it at the Public Quay just below the Bridge. So cautious were they, and so secretive that naturally the inhabitants of Crediton felt themselves at a disadvantage. Something was being planned which involved their town but excluded it from decision making, so they held a general protest meeting. They demanded that meetings of the canal promoters should be public and asserted that their ideas weren't sufficiently comprehensive anyhow. So they put forward a few of their own under a more grandiose title - The Public Devonshire Canal. This was a scheme for a canal to start at Coleford near Colebrooke and run past Crediton to the canal which was under consideration at that time, - the Grand Western canal near Topsham. Enthusiastic spirits at this meeting suggested further extensions northwards to North Tawton and even farther, and substantial subscriptions were promised. At a later meeting even more ambitious schemes were put forward, namely a canal from Topsham to Barnstaple bisecting the county, with subsidiary branches to Exeter and North Tawton. Elaborate surveys were made and revenue estimates produced.

Lime and sea sand, clay, cider, timber, woollen goods, coal and iron - the last two the optimistic gentlemen hoped to find en route during the necessary excavations. The carriage of all these commodities would provide, in their opinion, and income of nearly £12,000 a year. Unfortunately it did not. In fact there was no income because there was no canal. In two years the whole wildly extravagant plan had been dropped, although there was sufficient militancy left in the movement to animate protests against the Exeter - Crediton ideas when they were put forward once more, and to try to off-set Lord Rolle's Torrington canal with one of their own.

Meanwhile the early efforts of the Exeter gentlemen faded, and war pushed them further into the background, but in 1800 the proposed line and methods of construction were again considered and in 1801 the original line was authorised. Adequate capital was forthcoming, Exeter Corporation becoming one of the subscribers, and a reciprocal arrangement was entered into for the use of both canals. Running from the basin at Exe Bridge the line was to be taken above it round the weirs by Exwick and on to Cowley Bridge, then up the valley of the Creedy; using both rivers where necessary, a distance of eight miles. Matters remained static after the official formation of the company until 1808 when land was purchased, also some buildings, at Newton St. Cyres. In 1810 a small stretch of the proposed line was excavated above the bridge to the extent of approximately half a mile. This is still usefully employed as a flood relief channel. The company's endeavours were totally exhausted by this effort and in 1818 the scheme was finally abandoned, the company coming to an end about 1822.

Canal Ambitions at Ashburton

With canals being proposed everywhere Ashburton did not intend to be left out of things. Unfortunately the promoters of a canal in that district had determined opponents in the trustees of the North End Totnes turnpike road. When the canal enthusiasts appeared to have overcome their initial difficulties, which were mainly financial, and seemed in a fair way to succeed, the turnpike men called a meeting to discuss the best way to object to the canal scheme which they feared would affect the revenue of the turnpike road. In a small place it is easy to make enemies but not so easy to deal with them. The canal men, finding the trustees so determined to oppose their scheme, abandoned it after they had lodged a scheme for a canal from the Dart above the Bridge at Totnes to Ashburton, rising over two hundred feet by twentyfour locks.

Cann Quarry Canal

In 1778 a survey was made by the famous Smeaton, for

a canal from the slate quarries at Plympton to the Marsh Mills bridge over the Plym. This was required by John Parker afterwards Lord Boringdon. Smeaton proposed a canal of a little over two miles in length, falling thirty feet by locks, but honestly suggested that a railway could be built at half the cost and in a much shorter time. Nothing more was done about the plan for the canal at that time, but forty years later the then Earl of Morley the new title of the Parker family head, became involved with the Dartmoor Railway over a question of carriage. Perhaps rather ostentatiously he began to construct a small waterway about six feet in width from the Plym valley to Marsh Mills. This was merely a weapon to influence the lowering of tolls by the railway company and when agreement was reached for the carriage of his slate the Earl left off canal building.

River Taw at Rock Park, Barnstaple.

Proposed Braunton Canal

A Bill to authorise a drainage and enclosure scheme was proposed in 1810 which was to include a canal to run from Wrasenton Marsh to lime kilns at the upper end of Yellaton, and from there to the famous Braunton Field. The Act was passed in due course but the canal was omitted from it. However the two drainage channels made in the Marsh suggested the idea of a navigable channel to James Green who, in 1821 deposited plans for a scheme, but unfortunately nothing further transpired. In 1845 a canal was proposed which would run from Barnstaple to Umberleigh using the Taw, but this also began and ended with the survey.

The Grand Western Canal

This was largely a Somerset proposal although the original scheme was a very grand affair by which the canal was to run from Topsham up the valley of the Clyst, with a short extension to Sowton, then on into the Culm valley, passing Cullompton and providing a short branch to it, then continuing to Tiverton passing south of Sampford Peverell. Two reservoirs were to provide extra water from Culmstock and two more just past Burlescombe and to the north, provided another feeder. The canal was then to run on into Somerset, the whole undertaking to cost an estimated £166,-000. Much discussion, proposals and counterproposals, followed the preliminary meeting at Cullompton in 1792 and different surveys were made by independent engineers. In 1794 however, Exeter Corporation raised its voice. The Exeter canal also carried coal which was the suggested main traffic for the Grand Western, and the Corporation feared a loss of revenue. In addition the idea of taking water from the Culm was frowned upon as likely to cause trouble for the city water supply. The Grand Western company had to relinquish the idea of a branch of the canal to Sowton and to undertake to divert its coal cargoes to Topsham so that Exeter could claim dues for the use of its canal, making the coal traffic more expensive.

Eventually an Act authorising the construction of the canal was passed in 1796. It was to be just over thirtysix miles long with branches to Tiverton and Cullompton and reservoirs at Hemyock and Lowdwells. So far so good, but rising prices, national conditions and the war all had their effect and the canal scheme was shelved for some considerable time. By the time enthusiasm for the canal had once more arisen, difficulties in company policy were experienced. The Kennet & Avon Company were invited to assist but refused, although eventually a few of that company's shareholders did come to the aid of the Grand Western, and in 1810 the canal was started at its summit level at Holcombe. In August 1814 it was opened as far as Tiverton.

Meanwhile the Bristol & Taunton company had been revived under the name of the Bridgewater & Taunton company and a scheme for a new canal from Taunton to Lowdwells was put forward which included an extension of the old one to the Exeter canal. The idea was unenthusiastically received and for some years the company was bedevilled by construction and financial difficulties but by 1841 it had achieved a modest success. However by then the railways had come to Devon and in 1844 the Bristol and Exeter Railway had been started, reducing the canal company's revenue for the following year by over a third. Receipts continued to fall and in 1864 the undertaking was sold. The short section west of the lock at Lowdwells was allowed to dry, the remaining section to Tiverton being left in commission for stone traffic, but this came to an end about 1924 and in 1962 the British Transport Commission abandoned the canal.

Tamar Manure Navigation

In 1793 several local businessmen and landowners met in Tavistock to consider the possibility of constructing a canal from the Tamar through Tavistock to the canal which was intended to reach Okehampton, the illfated Public Devonshire canal. Great enthusiasm was aroused so far afield as Exeter, the promoters of each canal attending the meetings of both companies. Surveys were made and reports and estimates prepared. When the scheme came before parliament over half the estimated cost had already been raised. Some work was done, mainly dredging and improving the river but although the company gave notice in 1810 of its intention to introduce a bill for extending the river navigation to join its proposed canal at Dunterton, nothing further was done. Coal and mining materials continued to be carried by the company, but rail and road carriage gradually super-

The River Tamar.

seded the water transport which declined until in the late nineteen twenties it ceased altogether. During the Second World War the Tamar Manure Navigation Company went into liquidation.

The Tavistock Canal

This was a short canal of only four miles, but in its time a very important waterway indeed. In 1803 it was proposed that a canal should be built from the Tavy at Tavistock to the Tamar at Morwellham, which would include a branch to the quarries operating at Mill Hill. The main traffic was in copper ore from Wheal Friendship and Wheal Crowndale, and merchandise in general to and from Tavistock. The Duke of Bedford who owned all the land concerned, approved of the idea and the line of the little canal was finally decided upon. There was to be an aquaduct over the river Lumburn, and a tunnel of over two thousand yards length through Morwelldown; the inclined plane which carried the trucks from the waterway to the quay had a fall of two hundred and thirty seven feet. Skilfully planned so that the current could drive mills as well as assist the speed of the boats it carried, the canal was started in 1803. With an eye to business the company stipulated that it should have the right to work all mineral lodes encountered during excavation, paying the Duke of Bedford one tenth of the proceeds. The Duke agreed, took up some shares, and gave the land for the canal. It is significant that the engineer in charge of the work was the young manager of the Wheal Friendship. When the tunnel through Morwelldown was started the excavators came upon a lode of copper which was developed at Wheal Crebor, a mine which produced up to 3,000 tons of copper annually during the first years of its existence. Mining and canal building went along amicably enough until 1812 when the pressures became too great and separate companies were formed.

Tavistock Canal at Fitzford.

The tunnelling through Morwelldown was a slow laborious business with about forty men working on it at once. Water had to be pumped out and bad air made conditions difficult, but finally in 1816 the canal was finished and ready for work. A large crowd of local people embarked in several iron boats or barges and were conveyed through the famous tunnel. A salute of twenty one guns was fired and music feasting and dancing continued until late in the day.

Unfortunately the slump which followed the French wars had begun to make itself felt and although the company carried out the final plan to build an extension to the slate quarries, business was bad enough to compel the lowering of charges. The mining and canal interests, although carried on separately, were managed by the same proprietors and in 1828, the mining side having got into difficulties, it was arranged that the mines should be run by those of the company wishing to interest themselves in the mining concern, the expenses of which should be their responsibility, while the canal profits should be distributed amongst all the proprietors. The mining company was wound up a year later.

The profits of the canal continued to decrease until 1845 when heavily reduced tolls stabilised matters to some extent. The famous Devon Consols Mine increased its output which meant that wharfage at Morwellham had to be increased to accommodate the increasing number of ships. In 1859 the South Devon and Tavistock Railway came to Tavistock and to enable the canal to compete with the railway the Duke of Bedford was requested to consider lowering the tolls charged for the use of the quays at Morwellham. There is no record that he did so. The proprietors then suggested selling their shares in the canal to the Duke for £10 a share which his Grace refused. Finally in 1872 the Duke offered £8 a share and half the cost of the requisite act transferring the canal to his ownership. From then on the little canal seemed to have been allowed to fall into disuse, but in the nineteen thirties it was dredged and an extension made to a reservoir from which a pipe conducted the water down the cliff to Morwellham to provide electric current by means of a hydro electric plant.

L'enuou

In Devon there is famous fishing, sailing and boating, surfing, bathing and quiet wandering along canal or riverside. Taking fishing first, the angling holiday maker can do no better than to write to the Devon River Authority for its extremely useful brochure. The address is County Hall Exeter. This brochure gives details of fish and the rivers and ponds and reservoirs where they can be caught. Salmon and brown and sea trout are in most of the larger rivers. Coarse fishing can be had in the ponds, both at Newton Abbot and in the Ilfracombe area. For sea fishing, although useful catches can be had on the north coast, (Welcombe Mouth near Hartland usually yields some good bass) the most prominent angling resort is Teignmouth where the annual angling festival is held every August. Practically every species of sea fish obtainable in British waters can be taken here, including shark. Plymouth also has an enthusiastic angling club as have most of the resorts, and visiting holiday makers are generally made most welcome. The addresses can be obtained from the publicity department of the local council of your chosen resort. For the Tamar and rivers flowing into it the Cornwall River Authority should be consulted.

Surfing is generally a sport of the north Devon resorts but for lazing about on the sands with an occasional dip in the sea, the south coast resorts are preeminent. Water ski-ing can be enjoyed at practically all of them. The serious swimmer will realise that local knowledge must be consulted before entering the sea, but for the holidays-only type of bather it cannot be too strongly emphasised that notices concerning the safety of beaches, times for bathing etc., must be taken seriously. It does not follow that because one end of a beach is safe the other is also; people who live in a place know it and its dangers better than anyone else. The warnings are there for the visitor's safety and must be obeyed.

The same also applies to boats. If you are in the least doubtful about your sailing prowess, hire a boat with a boatman. All kinds of craft can be hired at the various resorts. There are yacht clubs for the serious sailing man where visitors are usually welcome, and for those preferring to take a less strenuous voyage pleasure craft take passengers around the bays and up the rivers. Dartmouth has a particularly pleasant trip up the Dart to Totnes and river boats also take sightseers up the Teign from Teignmouth, while Plymouth runs regular passenger craft on the Tamar.

For the holiday maker delighting in quiet days by the river or canal, watching the fish rise and the waterbirds going about their business, Devon provides ideal conditions. The wide estuary of the Plym near Plympton harbours innumerable varieties of water fowl. A path runs beside the water and grassy banks afford comfortable reclining places for the indolent. Dartmoor provides many fussy little rivers where the brisker and smaller water birds live. The little dipper is a familiar sight here, perching on a stone in midstream in his handsome black and white plumage.

If you want to spend a holiday watching the big ships go by, then Plymouth is an obvious choice, but ships go up the Exeter canal too, though may be not such big ones. Tavistock canal is still in good order (though most of the others have silted or dried up,) but there are no boats using it now. The nature lover must certainly make a point of going to Slapton Lea and there are nature reserves in other parts of the county just as delightful. Beaches such as that at Wembury are controlled by the National Trust and are safe from exploitation. Particulars of them can be obtained from the Information Offices of the various councils, the Tourist Board, or the Head office of the Trust itself.